Rothesay Castle stands in the centre, and St Mary's Church on the southern edge, of the town of Rothesay, on the island of Bute. The island can be reached by ferry from Wemyss Bay or Colintraive.

Rothesay Castle
and St Mary's Church

Denys Pringle

Edited by Chris Tabraham
Illustrated by David Simon
Photography by Historic Scotland Photographic Unit
Designed by Magnus Design
Produced by Roy Stewart Print Services
from Sustainable Materials
Printed in Scotland by Buccleuch Printers Ltd., Hawick

First published by Historic Scotland 1995
Reprinted 2000
Copyright © Historic Scotland 1995
ISBN 0 7480 0810 1

Introduction

'*And they [the Norwegians] sailed to ... Bute. The Scots sat there in the castle, and a certain steward was one of the Scots...*
[The Norwegians] attacked the castle, but the Scots defended it, and they poured out boiling pitch. The Norwegians hewed the wall with axes, because it was soft... Many of the Norwegians fell, before they won the castle.'

(*SAGA OF HAAKON HAAKONSON*, RECALLING AN ATTACK ON THE CASTLE IN 1230)

Rothesay Castle is unique among Scottish castles both for its early date and unusual circular plan, and for its long and close association with the Stewarts, hereditary stewards of the Kings of Scots and from 1371 the royal house of Scotland. From them is descended Charles, Prince of Wales, the present Duke of Rothesay.

The present stone castle, of unusual circular plan, was probably begun in the first quarter of the thirteenth century by Walter, the third Steward. Bute had only a generation or two before being seized by the Scots from the King of Norway, who in 1230 and 1263 sent expeditions to retake it. Both ended in failure, and in 1266, when the island was formally confirmed as belonging to Scotland, the castle was strengthened by the addition of four rounded projecting towers and a gatehouse to the north, facing the sea.

The marriage of Walter Stewart to Robert the Bruce's daughter, Marjorie, resulted in 1371 in the Stewarts obtaining the throne, through Marjorie's son, Robert. Both Robert II (1371-90) and his son, Robert III (1390-1406), spent time at Rothesay Castle. The next monarch to take a personal interest was James IV (1488-1513), who seems to have begun the building of the large residential gatehouse that dominates the present approach. The work was finished under James V in 1540-2. In 1685 the castle was burned by the Duke of Argyll and abandoned as a lordly residence.

In 1816-8, the second Marquess of Bute had the courtyard cleared of vegetation and rubble; in 1871-9, the third Marquess cleared the moat and engaged the architect, William Burges, to restore the masonry. In 1900, the third Marquess also reconstructed the great hall in the gatehouse. Since 1961, the castle has been in State care.

An aerial view of Rothesay Castle from the north-west, showing the original circular curtain wall, the four projecting round towers, the gatehouse, and the chapel inside the courtyard. (Courtesy of the Royal Commission on the Ancient and Historical Monuments of Scotland.)

The Story of Rothesay Castle

THE NORSE BACKGROUND

In the early Middle Ages Bute, along with Arran and the Cumbraes, occupied a significant position on the border between two kingdoms: the westward-expanding kingdom of Scotland and the Norse kingdom of Man and the Isles (or Sodar and Man), ruled by the King of Norway.

Bute had probably been settled by pagan Norsemen around the end of the eighth century. Archaeological finds, as well as settlements containing longhouses, indicate a Norse presence persisting well into the twelfth century.

In 1158, however, the Manx king's authority in western Scotland and the Isles was successfully challenged by a Celto-Norse lord of Argyll named Somerled. On Somerled's death, in 1164, his inheritance was divided. The Outer Isles returned to Manx control, and Argyll and the Inner Isles were divided between his sons. It was possibly then that William the Lion, King of Scots (1165-1214), seized control of Bute and the islands in the Firth of Clyde.

THE STEWARTS

By around 1200, Bute was being held by Alan, William I's 'steward'. Alan's family was of Anglo-Norman origin. His grandfather had served as the steward of the Lords of Dol in Brittany before crossing to England, and his father, Walter I, had entered the service of David I, King of Scots, around 1136, becoming his steward. This important position in the royal household was both hereditary and honorific. By 1200, the family had extensive possessions in southern Scotland. Through such families of incomers David I and his successors introduced into Scotland the 'feudal system', whereby lords and barons were granted extensive tracts of land in return for performing military service for the King when required. A product of the feudal system introduced into Scotland at the same time was the castle, which not only served as the fortified residence of a lord but also symbolised the status of those to whom the King had entrusted control of an area.

Being a newly-won territory in a frontier zone, Bute was probably provided with a castle soon after its annexation; but who built it and when are uncertain. The site chosen for the castle was close by the seashore in Rothesay Bay, midway down the east coast of the island and within easy reach of the other Stewart lands across the Clyde. The earliest Stewart castles on the mainland, like Renfrew and Dundonald, seem to have been of earth and timber. The same may also have been the case at Rothesay, which could account for the castle's unusual rounded shape.

By 1230, however, the castle's outer wall had been built up in stone; a simple rounded-arch gateway gave access on the north, facing the sea, and a smaller postern gate, for emergency use, faced westward. This work may have been carried out by Alan's son, Walter II (1204-41).

The family tree of the Stewarts associated with Rothesay Castle

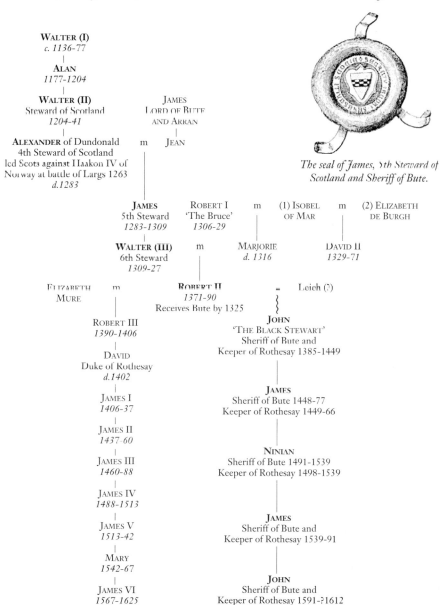

WALTER (I)
c. 1136–77

ALAN
1177–1204

WALTER (II)
Steward of Scotland
1204–41

JAMES
LORD OF BUTE
AND ARRAN

ALEXANDER of Dundonald
4th Steward of Scotland
led Scots against Haakon IV of
Norway at battle of Largs 1263
d.1283

m   **JEAN**

The seal of James, 5th Steward of
Scotland and Sheriff of Bute.

JAMES
5th Steward
1283–1309

ROBERT I
'The Bruce'
1306–29

m   (1) ISOBEL
OF MAR

m   (2) ELIZABETH
DE BURGH

WALTER (III)
6th Steward
1309–27

m   **MARJORIE**
d. 1316

DAVID II
1329–71

ELIZABETH
MURE

m

ROBERT II
1371–90
Receives Bute by 1325

=   Leich (?)

ROBERT III
1390–1406

JOHN
'THE BLACK STEWART'
Sheriff of Bute and
Keeper of Rothesay 1385–1449

DAVID
Duke of Rothesay
d.1402

JAMES I
1406–37

JAMES
Sheriff of Bute 1448–77
Keeper of Rothesay 1449–66

JAMES II
1437–60

JAMES III
1460–88

NINIAN
Sheriff of Bute 1491–1539
Keeper of Rothesay 1498–1539

JAMES IV
1488–1513

JAMES V
1513–42

JAMES
Sheriff of Bute and
Keeper of Rothesay 1539–91

MARY
1542–67

JAMES VI
1567–1625

JOHN
Sheriff of Bute and
Keeper of Rothesay 1591–?1612

THE NORWEGIANS ATTACK

The need for a castle on Bute was soon demonstrated. In 1230, Haakon IV of Norway appointed Uspak as King of Man and the Isles, and sent him to Bute with a fleet to claim his inheritance. *The Saga of Haakon Haakonson* relates:

> *'And they sailed south round the Mull of Kintyre, and so in to Bute. The Scots sat there in the castle; and a certain steward was one of the Scots. [The Norwegians] attacked the castle, but the Scots defended it, and they poured out boiling pitch. The Norwegians hewed the wall with axes, because it was soft. The torch-bearer who was called Skagi shot the steward to death. Many of the Norwegians fell, before they won the castle.'*

Other accounts say the siege lasted three days, and that the Norwegians 'bound over themselves shields of wood' in order to get close to the walls. Their success, however, was short-lived, for a fleet of nearly 200 ships under Alan of Galloway was sighted to the south. The Norwegians withdrew to Kintyre, where Uspak, who according to Scottish and Manx accounts had been struck by a stone during the fighting, died of his wound.

Rothesay returned to Scottish control. The breach in the castle's walls was quickly repaired, so that today it is impossible to tell exactly where it was.

In 1263 King Haakon himself led another expedition 'to avenge the warfare that the Scots had made in his dominions'. This time the Scots defending Rothesay Castle yielded it up in return for a truce; but once outside a number of them were slain.

The tide of history, however, began to turn against the Norsemen. Alexander III, King of Scots, refused to renounce his claim to Bute, Arran and the Cumbraes. Hakon, on the other hand, was well aware that the loyalty of the island leaders could not be guaranteed once his fleet left for home. As the autumn gales began, an inconclusive skirmish with Alexander Stewart's forces on the mainland shore at Largs in early November 1263 was the signal for withdrawal. Haakon died on the return journey at Kirkwall in Orkney. Three years later, in 1266, by the Treaty of Perth, his son, Magnus, handed over the kingdom of Man and the Isles to the Scottish King in return for a substantial payment.

Two successful Norwegian attacks on the castle had illustrated its inadequacies. It was probably at this point, when Bute became definitively part of the kingdom of Scotland, that its fortifications were upgraded by the addition of a projecting gatehouse containing a portcullis on the north, and four rounded projecting

An unusual stirrup-shaped arrow-slit in the splayed base of the south-east tower.

towers. The towers not only allowed archers, firing through carefully sited slits, to control the approaches, but also provided better domestic accommodation. The north-western tower was slightly larger than the others and probably contained the lord's private chambers; adjacent to it was the hall, built against the inside face of the wall and lit by south- or east-facing windows.

THE STEWARTS AND THE BRUCES

In 1296, when war broke out between Scotland and England, James the Stewart's sympathies lay throughout with the nationalist cause. In 1297, he was fully implicated in the revolt of William Wallace against the English occupation; and in February 1306, following Robert the Bruce's murder of John Comyn, Rothesay Castle was taken by sea and held for the Bruce cause by his associate, Robert Boyd of Cunningham. The Stewarts' connections with the Bruces were cemented by two marriages: the first, in 1302, between Robert Bruce himself and Elizabeth de Burgh, a niece of James the Stewart's wife, Egidia; and the second between Marjorie, Bruce's daughter from his first marriage, and Walter (III), James' son and heir.

In March 1316, by now pregnant, Marjorie fell from her horse, but in the hour of her death gave birth to a son, Robert, who in December 1318 was recognised as heir apparent. In March 1324, however, King Robert I's second wife also produced a son, David. Although still a minor, it was David II who became King on his father's death in 1329.

The Bute or Bannatyne Mazer, designed as a cup for circulating at ceremonial occasions. It is believed to have been made about 1316 for the Keeper of Rothesay Castle in honour of the High Steward of Scotland, and used in the castle.

THE STEWART SUCCESSION

When David II died in 1371, he was succeeded by his nephew, Robert II, first of a long line of Stewart monarchs to rule Scotland and, from 1603, England and Ireland also.

'King Bob' spent much of his time at Rothesay. From 1377 onwards, the exchequer accounts frequently record provisions, particularly wine, being sent there for the King's use. References to building works are few, though they are hinted at in the supply of wine 'for the king's work' in 1379 and wine and iron in 1381. In 1388, Hugh the Plumber was paid £6.13s.4d. for works to the castle; and in 1381 iron corselets, helmets, and other items of armour were bought. John of Fordun, writing between 1384 and 1387, described the castle as 'fair and impregnable'.

Robert II died at Dundonald Castle in Ayrshire in 1390 aged 74. He was succeeded by his son, John, who took the name Robert III. For much of his reign, however, the affairs of State were handled by his brother, Robert, Duke of Albany. The King's son, David, became Duke of Rothesay in 1398; but in 1401 on the advice of Albany he was confined in Falkland Palace, where he died in suspicious circumstances the following year. Some household expenses and a number of charters, including one granted to the burgh of Rothesay in 1401, show that Robert III spent some time in the castle. Bower's *Chronicle* even records that he died there, on Palm Sunday (4 April) 1406, and was buried in Paisley Abbey.

Rothesay Castle as it might have appeared in the sixteenth century, fr

JAMES IV (1488-1513) AND JAMES V (1513-42)

Between 1406 and 1488 there is little evidence for Kings of Scots taking much direct interest in Rothesay Castle though in 1469 the lordship of Bute, including the castle, was included by Act of Parliament in the patrimony of the monarch's eldest son, a tradition that still holds today. Under James IV, the place returned to prominence as a royal residence and stronghold. The principal reasons were strategic. The Western Isles, of which Bute historically formed a part, were still not fully subject to the King's authority. In May 1491 a parliamentary commission therefore met to examine 'the matter of the Ilis ... and to provide sua that the kingis lyegis may lif in quicte and peax'. The result was the forfeiture of John, Lord of the Isles, in May 1493, and the annexation of his lands to the Crown. But this did not immediately solve the problem of governing those remote regions.

reconstruction drawing prepared in the 1870s.

James attempted to impose his will on his newly-acquired domains by a series of naval expeditions. This brought him frequently to Rothesay. Only towards the end of his reign, however, are significant building works recorded there. From an entry made later in the account of the Chamberlain of Bute the work evidently related to the massive residential gatehouse, called *le dungeoun*, containing a porter's lodge and prison, a first-floor hall with two floors of chambers above, that was added on to the earlier gatehouse on the north side of the castle.

The works initiated by James IV probably continued after his unexpected death at Flodden in 1513 and into the reign of James V. The *Chronicle* of Robert Lindsay of Pitscottie credits the King's favourite, Sir James Hamilton of Finnart, with the completion in 1541 of certain building works at Rothesay for the sum of 3000 crowns. This work seems likely to have included the completion of the gatehouse, and the heightening of the two northern towers and the walls linking them to it. The present chapel in the courtyard may also have been built about this time. The date given by Pitscottie, however, cannot be correct, for Hamilton was executed for treason in August 1540.

THE LATER YEARS

Neither Mary Queen of Scots (1542-67) nor her son, James VI (1567-1625) is known to have visited Rothesay. The castle continued to be lived in and maintained by its hereditary Stewart captains and keepers.

In 1650, Rothesay Castle was garrisoned by Cromwellian troops; when they departed in 1659, they are said to have demolished part of the defences.

When James VII came to the throne in 1685, Archibald, ninth Earl of Argyll, led a short-lived revolt, during which Rothesay was plundered and the castle attacked and burned, making it uninhabitable. The Keeper, Sir James (IV) Stewart, and his family therefore moved from the now derelict castle to Mansion House, in Rothesay High Street (now the Bute Estates Office).

In 1716, Martin Martin described the castle as containing 'several little Houses within', besides the chapel. During the Napoleonic Wars the gatehouse was used as a powder magazine by the local volunteer force raised to defend Bute.

The north side of the courtyard before the restoration of 1872-9.
(Courtesy of the Royal Commission on the Ancient and Historical Monuments of Scotland.)

Between 1816 and 1818, the Keeper, John (VI) Crichton Stuart, second Marquess of Bute, employed 70 men to excavate the castle ruins and repair the vault over the gateway. The work was resumed by the estate factor, J R Thomson, for the third Marquess in 1871. The courtyard was excavated, revealing foundations of a number of buildings, a series of stone drains, and various cannon balls and iron weapons (now in Rothesay Museum). In 1872, a report on the castle was drawn up by the eminent English architect, William Burges. Following Burges's recommendations, the work at Rothesay, carried out between 1872 and 1879, consisted largely of consolidation rather than rebuilding. During the clearance of the moat, the lower portions of the original oak bridge were found, burnt down as far as the water level.

In 1900, the main hall on the first floor of the gatehouse was reconstructed. In 1937, part of the north-west or pigeon tower collapsed, and was skilfully rebuilt. In 1961, the Marquess of Bute placed the castle in State care.

John Crichton Stuart, 3rd Marquess of Bute.

The great hall looking north towards the fireplace.
The door on the left led to the latrine turret.

A Short Tour of

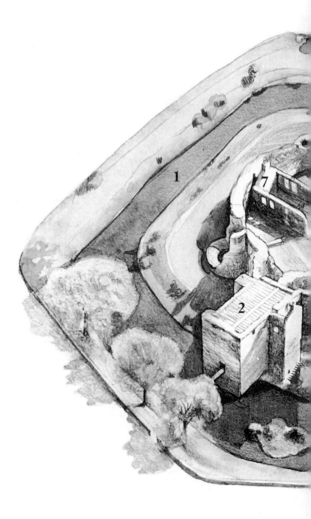

1. MOAT
A WATER-FILLED DEFENSIVE DITCH FILLED
BY A BURN FROM LOCH FAD. A TIMBER
PALISADE WOULD HAVE LINED THE INNER
EDGE OF THE MOAT.

2. GATEHOUSE
A LARGE RESIDENTIAL BUILDING ADDED TO
THE FRONT OF THE EARLIER GATE BY JAMES
IV AND JAMES V (1488-1542) TO PROVIDE MORE
FITTINGLY REGAL ACCOMMODATION.
ABOVE THE ENTRANCE PEND, PORTER'S
LODGE AND PRISON IS THE GREAT HALL,
LARGELY RESTORED BY THE 3RD MARQUESS
OF BUTE IN 1900.

3. COURTYARD
NOW A PLEASANT GRASSY AREA BUT IN
MEDIEVAL TIMES CROWDED WITH
BUILDINGS (EG FEASTING HALL, STABLES,
FORGE, GRANARY). THE WELL IS TO THE
NORTH-EAST.

4. CURTAIN WALL
A HIGH, THICK STONE WALL ENCLOSING
THE COURTYARD, BUILT C. 1200 USING
YELLOW AND RED SANDSTONE ASHLAR
BLOCKS, BUT HEIGHTENED C. 1500 USING
ANGULAR WHINSTONE RUBBLE. FOUR
PROJECTING ROUND TOWERS WERE ADDED
TO THE WALL AFTER THE LAST NORWEGIAN
ATTACK IN 1263, BOTH TO IMPROVE
DEFENCE AND ALSO TO PROVIDE MORE
DOMESTIC ACCOMMODATION.

Rothesay Castle

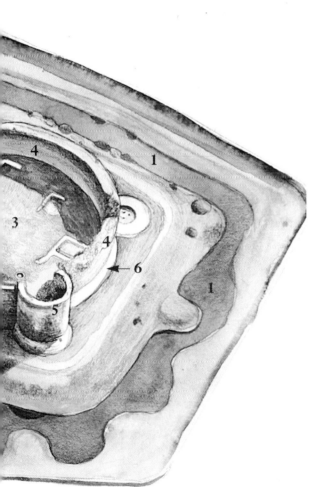

5. PIGEON TOWER

LARGER THAN THE OTHER THREE PROJECTING TOWERS AND PROBABLY ORIGINALLY HOUSING THE PRIVATE LODGING OF THE CASTLE'S OWNER UNTIL THE GATEHOUSE [2] WAS BUILT. THE TOP FLOOR WAS CONVERTED INTO A DOVECOT IN THE 16TH CENTURY.

6. POSTERN GATE

A NARROW SIDE GATE THROUGH THE 13TH-CENTURY CURTAIN WALL [4], LATER BLOCKED UP.

7. CHAPEL

PROBABLY BUILT C. 1500 AS PART OF THE REMODELLING OF THE CASTLE BY JAMES IV AND JAMES V AND DEDICATED TO ST MICHAEL THE ARCHANGEL, PATRON SAINT OF WARRIORS. THE CHAPEL ITSELF WAS ON THE FIRST FLOOR ABOVE A STORAGE BASEMENT. BEHIND THE CHAPEL ARE THE REMAINS OF A STAIR GIVING ACCESS TO A WALL-WALK.

Artist's bird's-eye view of the castle from the north-west.

The Architecture of Rothesay Castle

THE GATEHOUSE

The castle as it survives today is roughly circular in plan, some 42 m in diameter, with rounded towers projecting from the walls on the north-east, north-west, south-east and south-west quarters. A large rectangular gatehouse provides the sole means of access on the north. This gatehouse, referred to in 1518-20 as *le dungeoun*, was added to the front of an earlier gate by James IV and James V to provide more fittingly regal accommodation inside the castle.

The castle from the north-west with the c. 1500 gatehouse and latrine turret on the left and the thirteenth-century pigeon tower on the right. The curtain wall in between has preserved the outline of the original thirteenth-century crenellated (indented) battlements below later masonry.

The gate itself, surmounted by a panel displaying the royal arms, is set roughly in the centre of the gatehouse's north wall. It is reached across a water-filled **moat**, which surrounds the castle, by a modern timber **bridge**, whose foundations rest on those of the medieval bridge that were discovered when the moat was cleared in 1872-9. The final section of the medieval bridge evidently consisted of a drawbridge, for the rectangular recess into which this fitted when raised is plainly visible framing the **gate**. Behind it, an iron-grilled gate (or yett) would have been set into the rounded arch of the gate itself; and behind this stood a timber door, secured when shut by a draw-bar sliding out from a **slot** on the right-hand side.

The gate leads into a vaulted entrance passage, or **pend**. Immediately to the left is the door to the **porter's lodge** (now a toilet). The porter, or gatekeeper, was responsible not only for controlling who went in or out of the castle, but also for the warding of prisoners awaiting trial by the sheriff or visiting royal justices. Some prisoners would have been accommodated in chambers within the castle; but the more dangerous or untrustworthy types would have been confined in a **cell** below the gatehouse. The entrance to this is down a hatch a little further along the pend. The cell consists of a low vaulted room, and contains a latrine emptying into the moat. In 1489, Sir Patrick Lindsay was cast into a dark dungeon in the castle and told to 'sitt quhair he should not sie his feet for ane yeir'.

At the far end of the entrance pend, a door to the right leads out to the **lists**, or space between the castle wall and the timber palisade that would have lined the inner edge of the moat. It seems likely that there would originally have been another door in a similar position on the east. However, when the upper part of the gatehouse was rebuilt in 1900, a spiral staircase was inserted into this space.

The original **stair** to the first floor still exists inside the east wall of the gatehouse. It emerges towards the north end of what must have been the principal **hall** (the great hall) of the gatehouse. Unfortunately, by the 1870s most of the east and south walls of this room had gone; what we see now is largely the work of the third Marquess of Bute. The room was heated by a broad fireplace in the west wall. To its right is a window with seats, while to its left a door leads into a projecting **latrine turret**. Latterly this has been made into a small room with a window inserted on the west. Originally it was half its present size, with one of the two slits in the floor serving the latrines at this level, and the other behind it those of the floor above; both emptied down a chute into the moat.

To the south of the hall there seems to have been another smaller room. However, the original position of the wall dividing it from the hall is uncertain. A drawing made in 1872 shows remains of a fireplace in the west wall, and of a door at the head of the stone steps leading up from the courtyard. Other doors gave into the covered wall-walks leading to the two northern round-towers. This room would probably have housed the windlass for raising the portcullis. On its east side, a **spiral staircase**, once covered by a fine rib-vault, probably ascended to the upper floors.

The **second floor** and **garret** are now inaccessible to visitors but would appear to have contained several smaller chambers. The wall-head was surrounded by a parapet, carried forward on a single row of corbels. The latrine tower had a small room built over it, probably in the seventeenth century, with a crow-stepped gable wall on the west incorporating a fireplace and a chimney flanked by a pair of gun-loops.

At the foot of the modern spiral stair inside the gatehouse is a **guard room**, which at one time possibly served as a prison. It is covered by a barrel-vault, and dates from the sixteenth century. Its south wall represents the original outer wall of the castle, and its west wall the outer face of the first gate-tower, added after the Norse attack of 1230.

The sequence of castle gates is best seen inside the gate passage. The earliest **gateway**, nearest the courtyard, consisted of a single timber door, set behind plain chamfered stone jambs and secured by a draw-bar; the arch-head has gone, but the rear-arch, rebuilt in 1816-8, is elliptical. After 1230, a higher, pointed arch was added to the front of the gate. This too has been repaired in recent times, but the slot for a **portcullis** can still be seen in the surviving haunches of the original vault; quite possibly it was preceded by a slit-machicolation, through which defenders in the chamber above could have rained down missiles or boiling pitch on the heads of attackers attempting to approach the gate. In front of this was added, around 1512-42, *le dungeoun* already described. At that time, however, the end of the pend facing into the courtyard was narrowed and provided with a door preceded by a yett. Thus the gatehouse built by James IV and James V would have been defensible against attack both from outside the castle and from within.

The entrance passage, or pend, viewed from inside the courtyard. The original thirteenth-century entrance gate, in the foreground, was extended twice to achieve the long passage surviving today.

The Courtyard

The gate passage leads straight into the castle courtyard. Today this is a pleasant grassy area, a sun-trap on a summer's day; but in the Middle Ages it would have been quite different (see the reconstruction on pages 8-9). The excavations carried out in the nineteenth century revealed the foundations of a number of buildings packed into the enclosed space, including a **stable** and a blacksmith's **forge**. An elaborate system of stone-lined **drains** evidently represented an attempt to reduce the amount of mud and filth littering the areas between them. We may assume that these buildings, or their predecessors, would have included the granary and possibly byres housing the cattle paid as rent to the royal estates in Bute in the fifteenth century. None of the original thirteenth-century courtyard buildings remains, and no trace was found in the excavations. However, the location of the **feasting hall**, the chief public room in the castle, appears to be indicated by a row of joist pockets in the west wall, running south from the north-west tower at first-floor level. It seems likely that most of the medieval courtyard buildings were of timber.

The **curtain wall** surrounding the courtyard is essentially early thirteenth-century, built in yellow and red sandstone ashlar blocks. It was heightened in the early sixteenth century. On the inside the heightening is faced with angular whinstone rubble, similar to that on the lower part of the gatehouse, and on the outside with small white ashlar blocks. Between the gatehouse and the north-east and north-west towers, however, the heightening was carried out somewhat differently. Here the original thirteenth-century wall-head was retained, and the wall-walk was enclosed to form a passageway inside the wall, linking the gatehouse to the tower chambers. The split whinstone rubble masonry used for this heightening is similar to that of the upper part of the gatehouse, allowing it to be dated to James V's building works of around 1540.

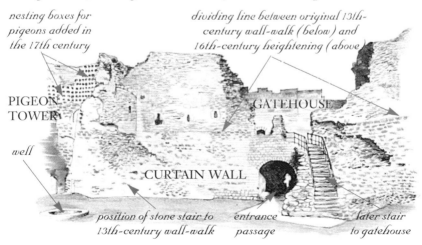

nesting boxes for pigeons added in the 17th century

dividing line between original 13th-century wall-walk (below) and 16th-century heightening (above)

PIGEON TOWER

GATEHOUSE

well

CURTAIN WALL

position of stone stair to 13th-century wall-walk

entrance passage

later stair to gatehouse

The north side of the courtyard.

In the thirteenth century, as in later periods, a **wall-walk** would have continued right around the top of the wall. Two sets of stone **stairs** leading up to it from ground level survive, one on the east (now obscured by the chapel) and one between the gatehouse and the north-west tower. Remains of stairs also survive at wall-head level, leading up to the tops of the two northerly towers. In the west wall is a narrow **postern gate**, now walled up on the outside.

The tower (known as the **pigeon tower**) that adjoined the north-west corner of the hall is somewhat larger and better preserved than the other towers, and probably contained the private chambers of the castle's owner. Originally it had three storeys, the ground and first floors, each of timber, corresponding to the floor levels of the adjoining hall block, and the upper floor reached from the wall-walk. The rooms at these levels were lit by tall arrow-slits with stirrup-shaped bases (see photograph on page 6). In the early sixteenth century, when the castle wall was heightened, an upper chamber was added to the tower. This was lit by a more spacious rectangular window and provided with a projecting latrine. The room was converted into a **dovecot** in the seventeenth century.

The north-west or pigeon tower, built in the thirteenth century to house the lord's private chambers, heightened c. 1500, and partially converted into a dovecot in the seventeenth century.

The other towers, less well preserved, seem to have contained domestic chambers for members of the household. An extra storey was added to the north-east tower in the sixteenth century. The south-west tower has mostly gone. Of the south-east tower only the splayed base remains though its domestic character is shown by a latrine closet set into the wall to the right of its ground-floor entrance.

THE CHAPEL

The only building within the courtyard to survive relatively intact is the chapel; a plain rectangular structure built against the inside face of the east wall. It had two storeys and a pitched roof, the floor and roof being of timber. The **ground floor**, lit by four barred and unglazed slit-windows, with a main door on the west and another at the south-east corner, seems to have been no more than a storage basement.

The **chapel** itself was on the **first floor**, and was reached by an external stone stair leading to a door at the west end of the south wall. Inside the door is a **stoup** for holy water, at the eastern end of the same wall is a *piscina*, set below a trefoil arch, where the sacred vessels used during mass were washed. A **cupboard**, or aumbry, is set into the east wall just north of where the altar would have stood. Each side wall contained three windows lighting the sanctuary. All the windows appear to have had internal timber shutters, and the door could be bolted from inside by a timber draw-bar.

It is probable that the castle would have contained a chapel from the time of its foundation. To judge by its architecture,

The south wall of the chapel with its once-fine traceried window.

however, the present building is unlikely to date earlier than the fifteenth century; indeed, its masonry is comparable to that of the upper part of the gatehouse, suggesting that it belongs to the phase of remodelling of the castle carried out by James IV and James V. In 1507, the dedication of the chapel is given as being to St Michael the Archangel, patron saint of warriors.

THE EXTERIOR

Before leaving, it is worthwhile taking a closer look at the outside of the castle by going out of the postern gate in the west side of the gatehouse and walking around the **lists**, or space between the walls and the moat.

Between the gatehouse and the pigeon tower the thirteenth-century **curtain wall** survives almost to its full height below the heightening carried out in the sixteenth century. The earlier masonry consists of small neat ashlars, regularly coursed, while the addition is in split whinstone rubble. In heightening the wall the sixteenth-century masons have preserved the original thirteenth-century **crenellations**, or indented wall-head parapet – a rare survival for Scotland, though paralleled in similar circumstances at Skipness Castle (Argyll). Two broad upstanding merlons may be seen, each pierced by an observation slit, and three narrower crenelles through which the archers on the wall-head would have fired off their weapons. To the right the parapet steps up towards the tower so as to provide protection for people ascending the stair to the tower top; this indicates that the crenellation dates from the same period as the tower, towards the end of the thirteenth century.

In what was probably a secondary phase, the crenellation was enclosed by a projecting timber **brattice**; four of the putlog holes associated with this may be seen just below the level of the crenelles. The brattice, or machicolation, would have overhung the wall and allowed the defenders to prevent attackers from approaching its base and undermining it as the Norse raiders had done in 1230. Three more holes just below these four putlogs represent the positions of the stone channels which drained the thirteenth-century wall-walk; these appear to have been re-used in the sixteenth century to drain the raised wall-head.

The castle from the west with the c. 1500 gatehouse and its projecting latrine turret in the centre, the thirteenth-century pigeon tower to the right and the moat in the foreground.

The same sequence of wall-head features, although less well preserved, can also be seen in the surviving curtain wall between the gatehouse and the north-east tower. Elsewhere the crenellations seem to have been destroyed before the heightening of the walls took place.

Beyond the pigeon tower, an exposure made at the base of the wall in the nineteenth century shows that the tower was a later addition to what would originally have been a tower-less circular castle. Above the exposure, in the angle between tower and curtain wall is a corbelled latrine that would have served the upper-storey chamber added to the pigeon tower in the time of James IV. When the tower was made into a dovecot, the opening of the fine rectangular window was reduced in size and provided with a projecting landing slab to allow the birds in and out.

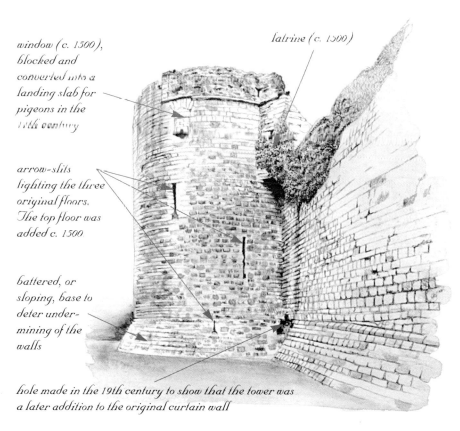

latrine (c. 1500)

window (c. 1500), blocked and converted into a landing slab for pigeons in the 19th century

arrow-slits lighting the three original floors. The top floor was added c. 1500

battered, or sloping, base to deter under-mining of the walls

hole made in the 19th century to show that the tower was a later addition to the original curtain wall

The north-west or pigeon tower and a stretch of curtain wall.

St Mary's Church, Rothesay

FROM CATHEDRAL TO PARISH CHURCH

*A*bout 1200AD the Island of Bute comprised a single parish, centred on St Blane's Church at Kingarth (in the south of the island). By the early fourteenth century, however, a second parish had been formed, based on St Mary's Church in Rothesay. This probably reflected the growing importance of the northern over the southern part of the island, brought about by the Scottish annexation of Bute and the establishment of Rothesay Castle. None the less, Bute remained technically subject to the Archbishop of Trondheim in Norway until 1472.

Although a rector of Rothesay is recorded in 1295, the church of St Mary is first mentioned in 1321, as the burial place of Alan, Bishop of Sodar (or Man and the Isles). His successor, Bishop Gilbert, was also buried there, suggesting that St Mary's served for a time as the cathedral church for the diocese.

In 1692, three years after the final disestablishment of episcopacy in Scotland, the nave of St Mary's was demolished and replaced by a building more suited to Presbyterian worship. This in turn was replaced by the present church in 1795.

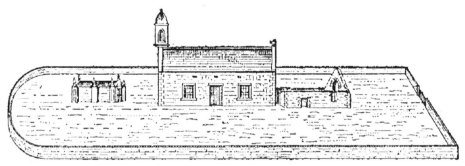

Rothesay Parish Church, as rebuilt in 1692, with the roofless chancel of St Mary's Church on the right and the Bute Mausoleum on the left. The seventeenth-century parish church was replaced by the present edifice in 1795.

THE CHANCEL

All that survives today of the medieval church is the ruined chancel with its fine three-light window with interesting tracery in the east gable. The **lancet windows** in the side walls and the design and location of the *piscina* (the basin for rinsing the altar vessels) and the **aumbry**, or cupboard, in the south wall, are closely comparable in style to the extension of the chancel of St Blane's, in the south of the island, indicating a date in the fourteenth century.

THE TOMBS

The most impressive features of the chancel are the monumental tombs. Their incumbents were evidently persons of importance, and their positions of honour, close to the altar, suggest that they may have been intended for the patron of the church and his lady. But who could they have been?

The **knight's tomb** is in the south wall. The effigy shows him in complete plate armour, his head resting on a jousting helmet crested with a dog's head, his feet on a lion. From the jewelled belt around his waist hang a sword and a dagger.

The **lady's tomb** (see page 24) is in the north wall. The effigy is at prayer dressed in a flowing gown and chaplet. Beside her lies a baby in a long robe. There are no armorials associated with the tomb and the significance of the eight rectangular panels, each with a man kneeling before a standing lady, is elusive.

The coat of arms on the knight's tomb indicates that he was connected by blood to the royal house of Stewart. One possibility is that Robert II (1371-90), the first Stewart monarch, built the tomb either for himself or for one of his ancestors. He himself could never have made use of it for he was buried at Scone. In the event, the tomb seems to have been used for others, probably the Stewart Sheriffs of Bute.

One of the grave-slabs on the floor has a badly-worn effigy of a knight, carved in the West Highland tradition and probably dating to the late fourteenth century.

The surviving chancel of St Mary's Church looking towards the east window. To the right of the window is a wall-cupboard, a piscina, *or arched basin, for rinsing the altar vessels, and the very fine knight's tomb. On the floor in the foreground is an effigy of a late-fourteenth-century knight.*

The lady's tomb in the north wall of the chancel of St Mary's Church.

Further Reading

ON THE CASTLE:

D MacGibbon and T Ross *The Castellated and Domestic Architecture of Scotland*, 1 (1887)

D MacGibbon and T Ross *The Ecclesiastical Architecture of Scotland*, 2 vols (1896-7)

W D Simpson 'The architectural history of Rothesay Castle', *Transactions of the Glasgow Archaeological Society*, 9 (1937)

ON ST MARY'S CHURCH:

J Mackinlay 'Accounts of two ancient monuments in the Church of St Mary, Rothesay', *Archaeologica Scotica*, III. i (1831)

J C Roger 'Notices of ancient monuments in the ruined Church of St Mary, Rothesay' *Proceedings of the Society of Antiquaries of Scotland*, 2 (1854-7), 466-81

ON BUTE GENERALLY:

J King Hewison *The Isle of Bute in the Olden Time*, 2 vols (1893-5)

D N Marshall *History of Bute*, revised edition (1992)

F A Walker & F J Sinclair *North Clyde Estuary: An Illustrated Architectural Guide* (1992)

ON CASTLES GENERALLY:

S Cruden *The Scottish Castle* (1981)

C Tabraham *Scottish Castles and Fortifications* (1990)

C Tabraham *Scotland's Castles* (1997)